HAUNTED HIS

T0012347

COASTER OF DEATH

by Leah Kaminski

Illustrations by Candy Briones

BEARPORT
PUBLISHING

Minneapolis, Minnesota

BEAR CLAW

Credits

22T: ©Francisco Goncalves/Getty Images; 22B: ©Internet Archive Book Images/Wikimedia

DISCLAIMER: This graphic story is a dramatization based on true events. It is intended to give the reader a sense of the narrative rather than a presentation of actual details as they occurred.

Library of Congress Cataloging-in-Publication Data is available at www.loc.gov or upon request from the publisher.

ISBN: 978-1-64747-014-2 (hardcover)
ISBN: 978-1-64747-021-0 (paperback)
ISBN: 978-1-64747-028-9 (ebook)

For more information, write to Bearport Publishing, 5357 Penn Avenue South, Minneapolis, MN 55419.
Printed in the United States of America.

CONTENTS

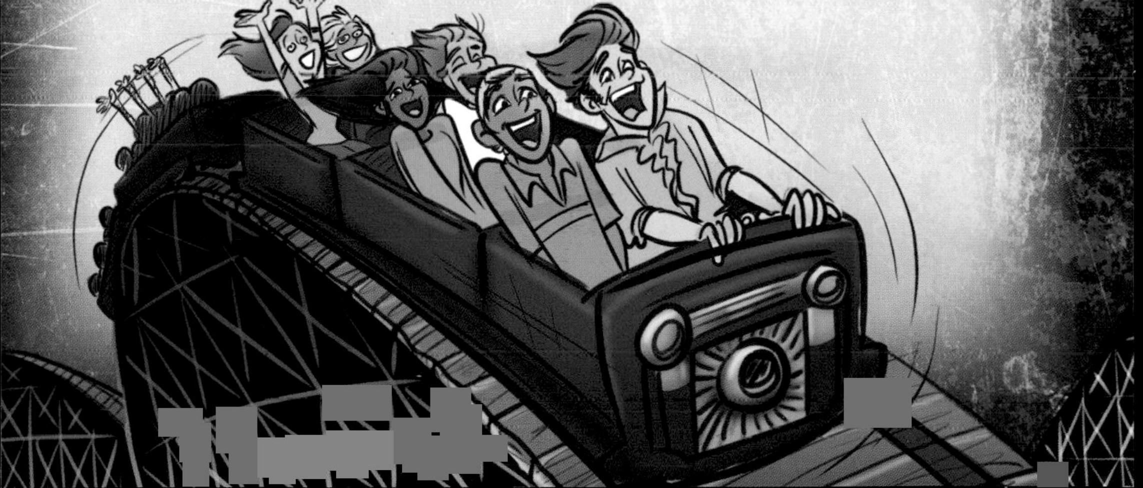

SCARY AMUSEMENT PARKS

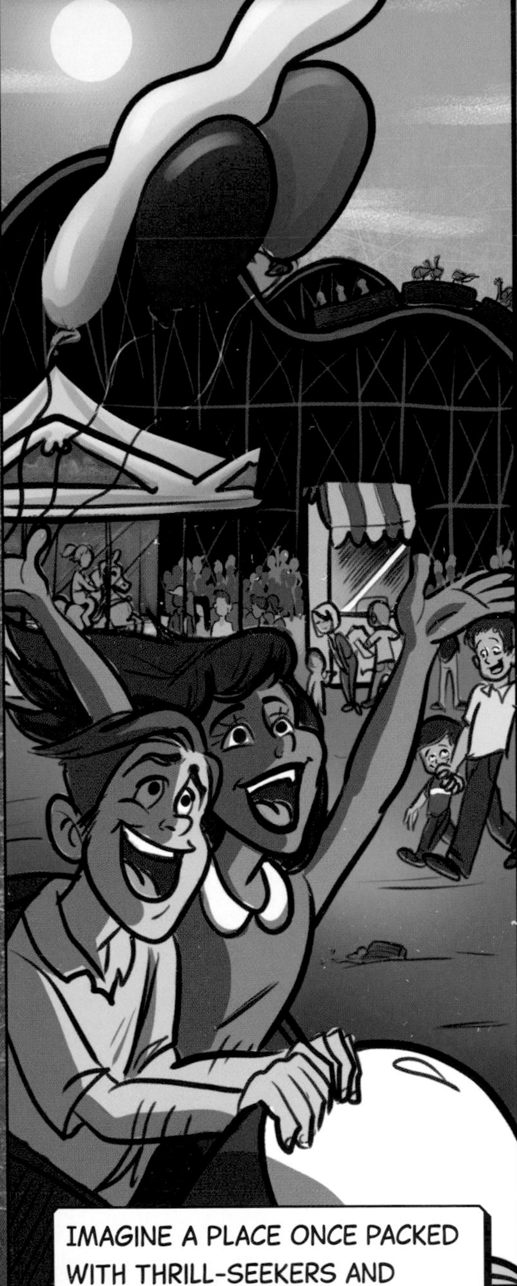
IMAGINE A PLACE ONCE PACKED WITH THRILL-SEEKERS AND FILLED WITH THE SOUND OF CHILDREN'S EXCITED LAUGHTER....

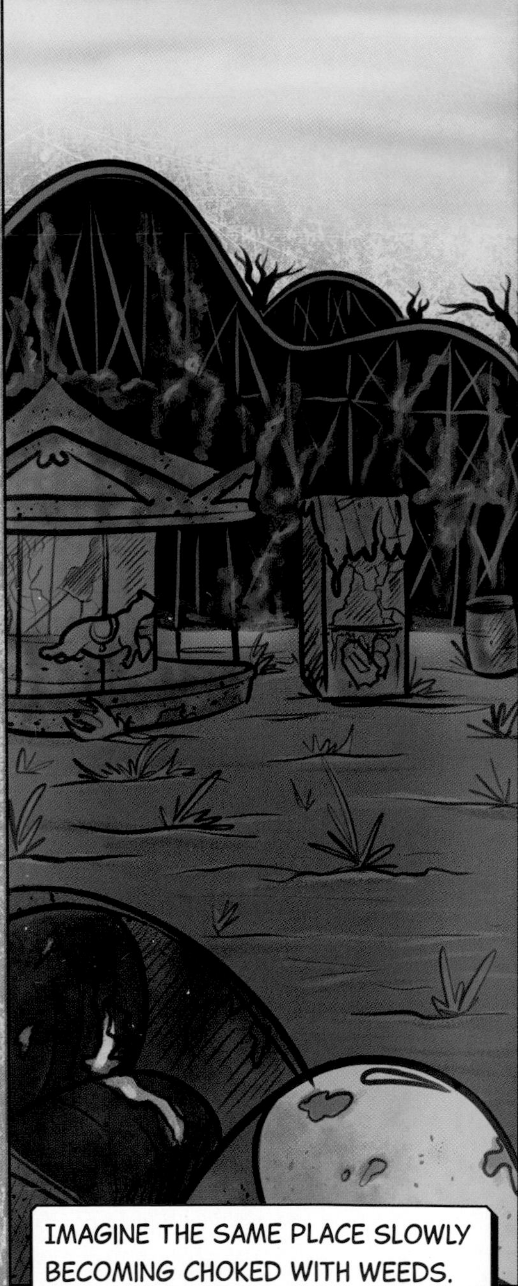
IMAGINE THE SAME PLACE SLOWLY BECOMING CHOKED WITH WEEDS. NOW, IT IS FILLED WITH THE QUIET CREAKING OF RUSTED METAL.

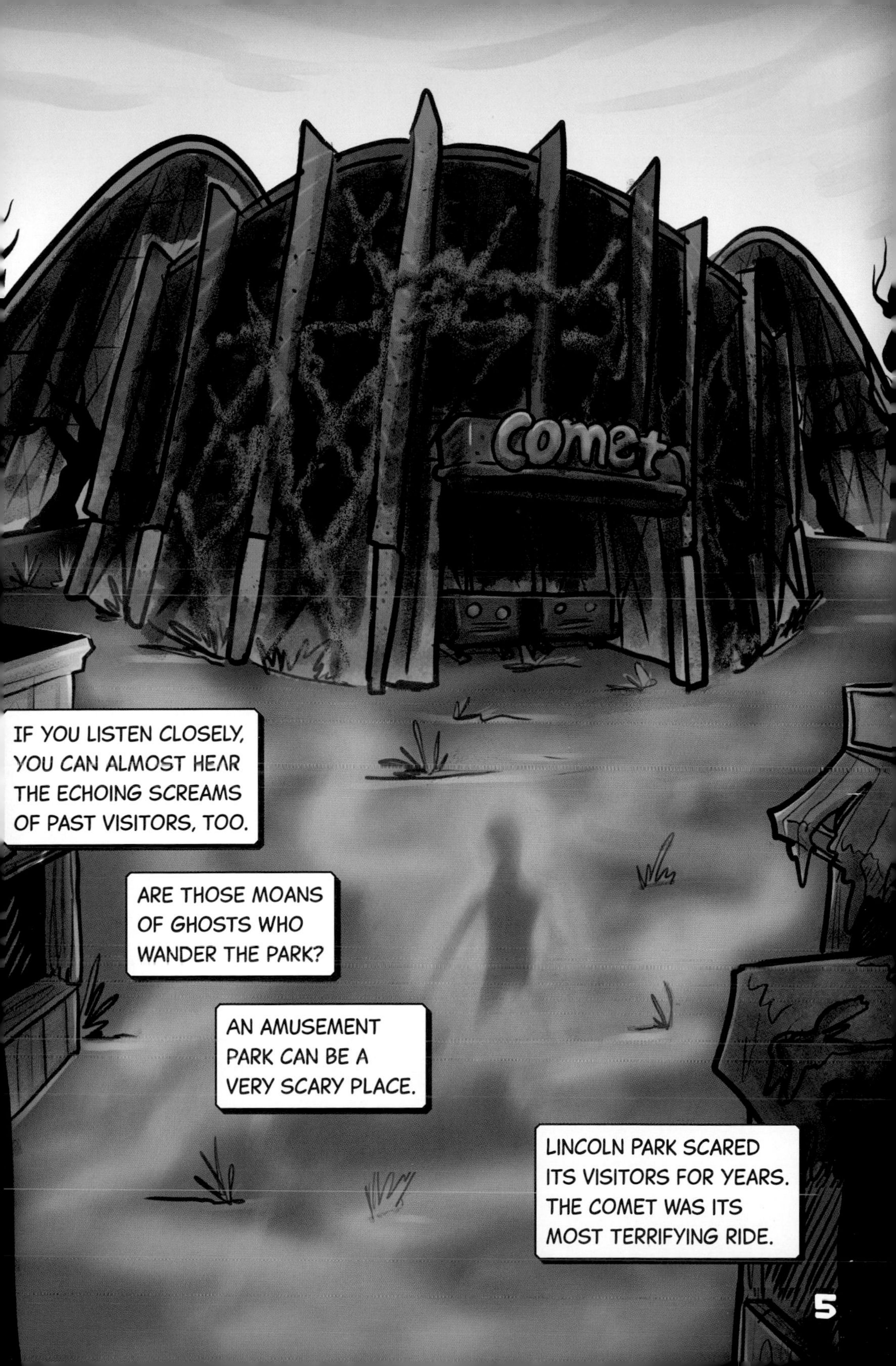
Comet
IF YOU LISTEN CLOSELY, YOU CAN ALMOST HEAR THE ECHOING SCREAMS OF PAST VISITORS, TOO.
ARE THOSE MOANS OF GHOSTS WHO WANDER THE PARK?
AN AMUSEMENT PARK CAN BE A VERY SCARY PLACE.
LINCOLN PARK SCARED ITS VISITORS FOR YEARS. THE COMET WAS ITS MOST TERRIFYING RIDE.

THE FIRST VICTIMS

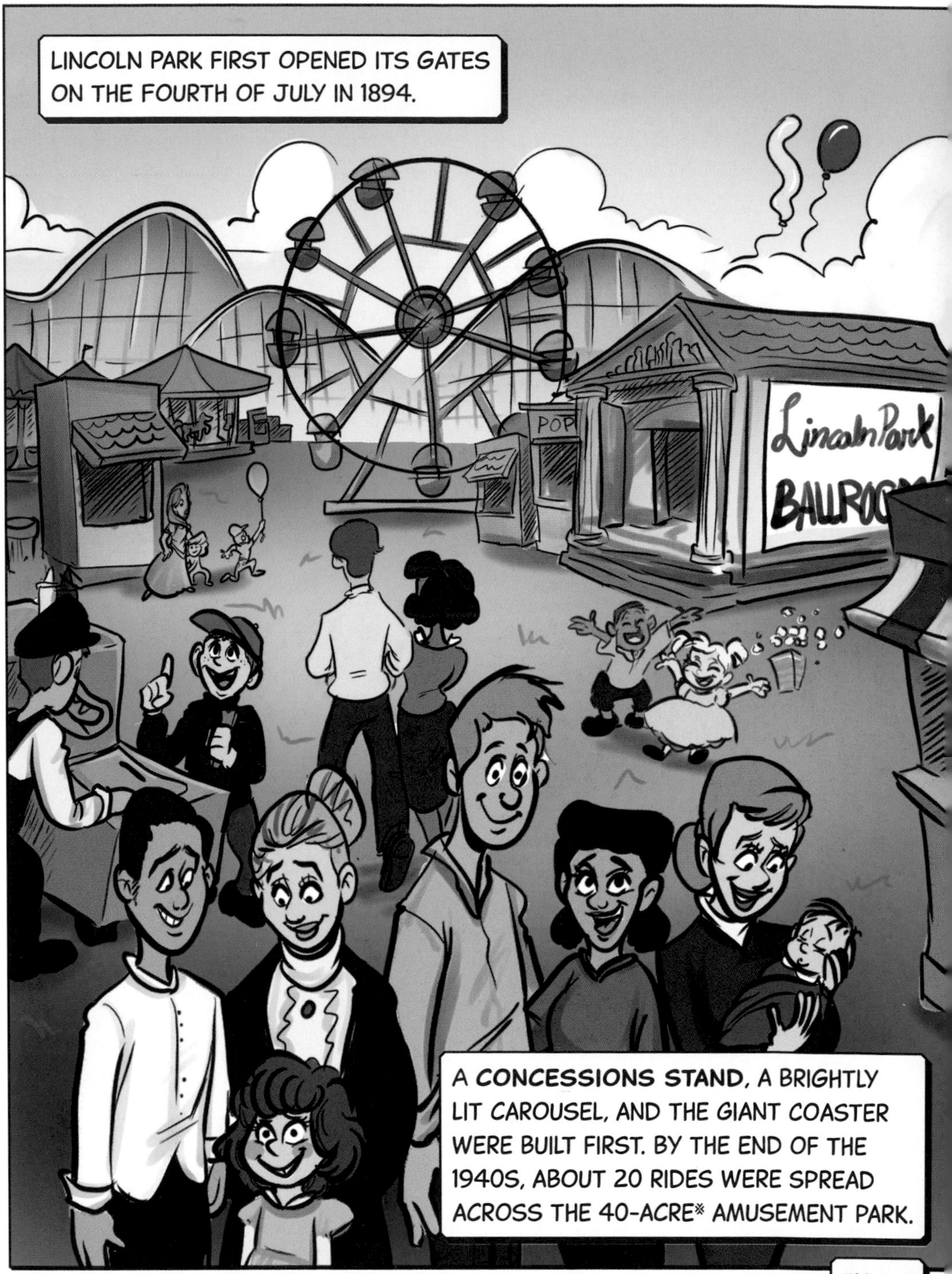
LINCOLN PARK FIRST OPENED ITS GATES ON THE FOURTH OF JULY IN 1894.
POP
Lincoln Park
A **CONCESSIONS STAND**, A BRIGHTLY LIT CAROUSEL, AND THE GIANT COASTER WERE BUILT FIRST. BY THE END OF THE 1940S, ABOUT 20 RIDES WERE SPREAD ACROSS THE 40-ACRE* AMUSEMENT PARK.

*16-HA

LINCOLN PARK BECAME VERY POPULAR. ITS CROWN JEWEL WAS THE COMET, A WOODEN ROLLER COASTER BUILT IN 1946.

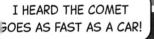

I HEARD THE COMET GOES AS FAST AS A CAR!

YES, AND IT FLIES 65 FEET※ INTO THE AIR!

※20 M

I'M SO EXCITED TO RIDE THE COMET!

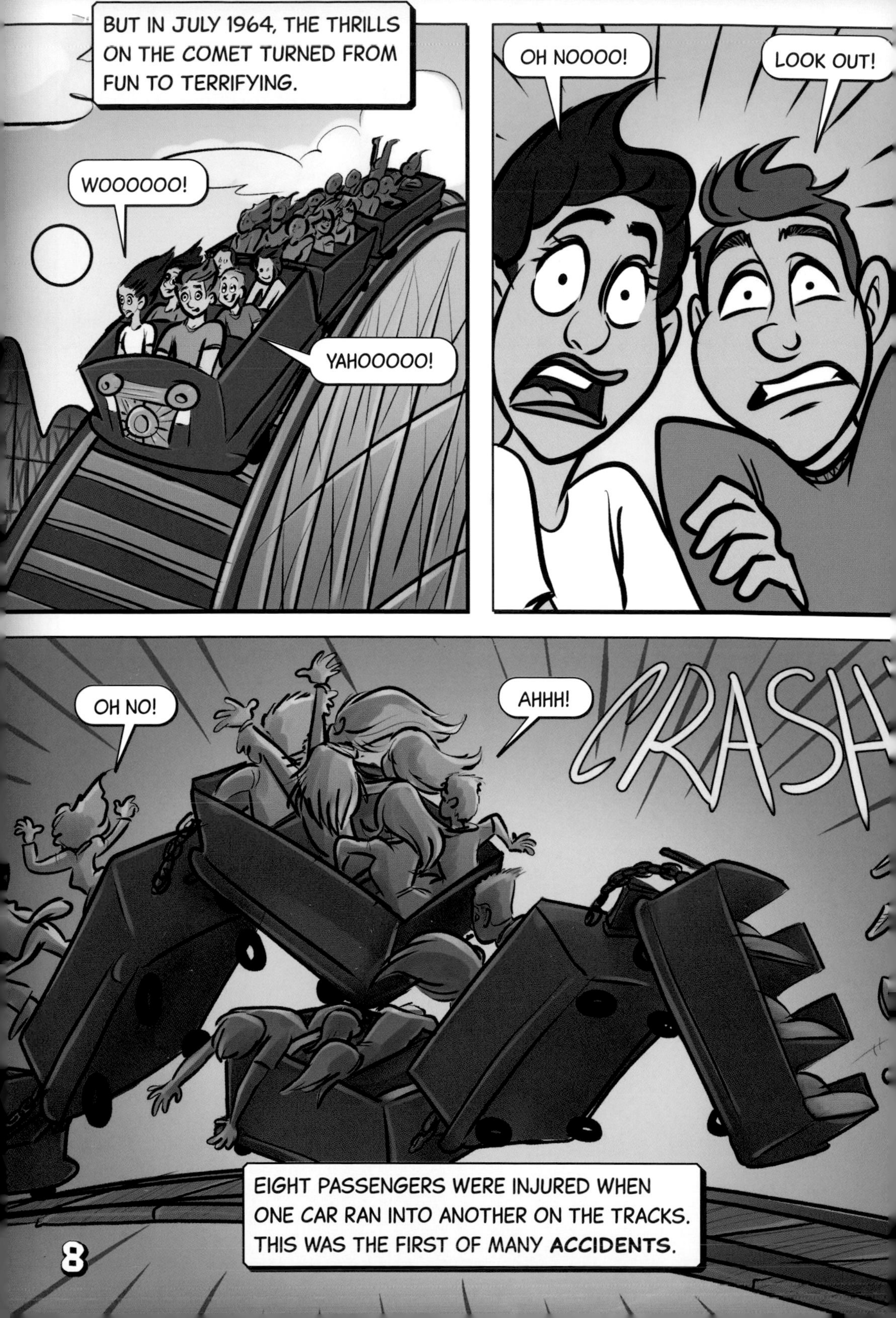
BUT IN JULY 1964, THE THRILLS ON THE COMET TURNED FROM FUN TO TERRIFYING.
WOOOOOO!
YAHOOOOO!
OH NOOOO!
LOOK OUT!
OH NO!
AHHH!
CRASH
EIGHT PASSENGERS WERE INJURED WHEN ONE CAR RAN INTO ANOTHER ON THE TRACKS. THIS WAS THE FIRST OF MANY **ACCIDENTS**.

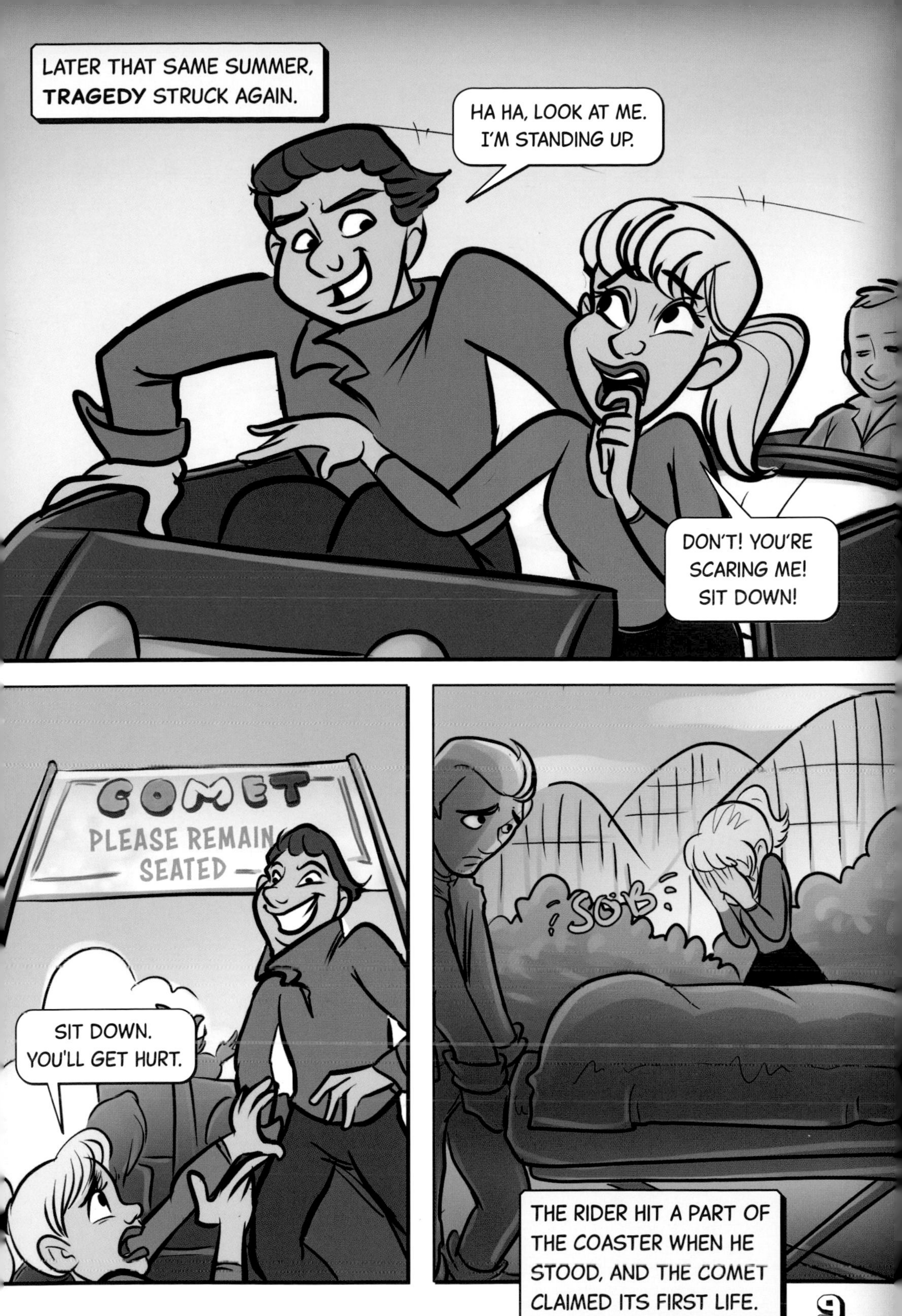
LATER THAT SAME SUMMER, **TRAGEDY** STRUCK AGAIN.
HA HA, LOOK AT ME. I'M STANDING UP.
DON'T! YOU'RE SCARING ME! SIT DOWN!
COMET
PLEASE REMAIN SEATED
SIT DOWN. YOU'LL GET HURT.
SOB
THE RIDER HIT A PART OF THE COASTER WHEN HE STOOD, AND THE COMET CLAIMED ITS FIRST LIFE.

A BLOODY SUMMER

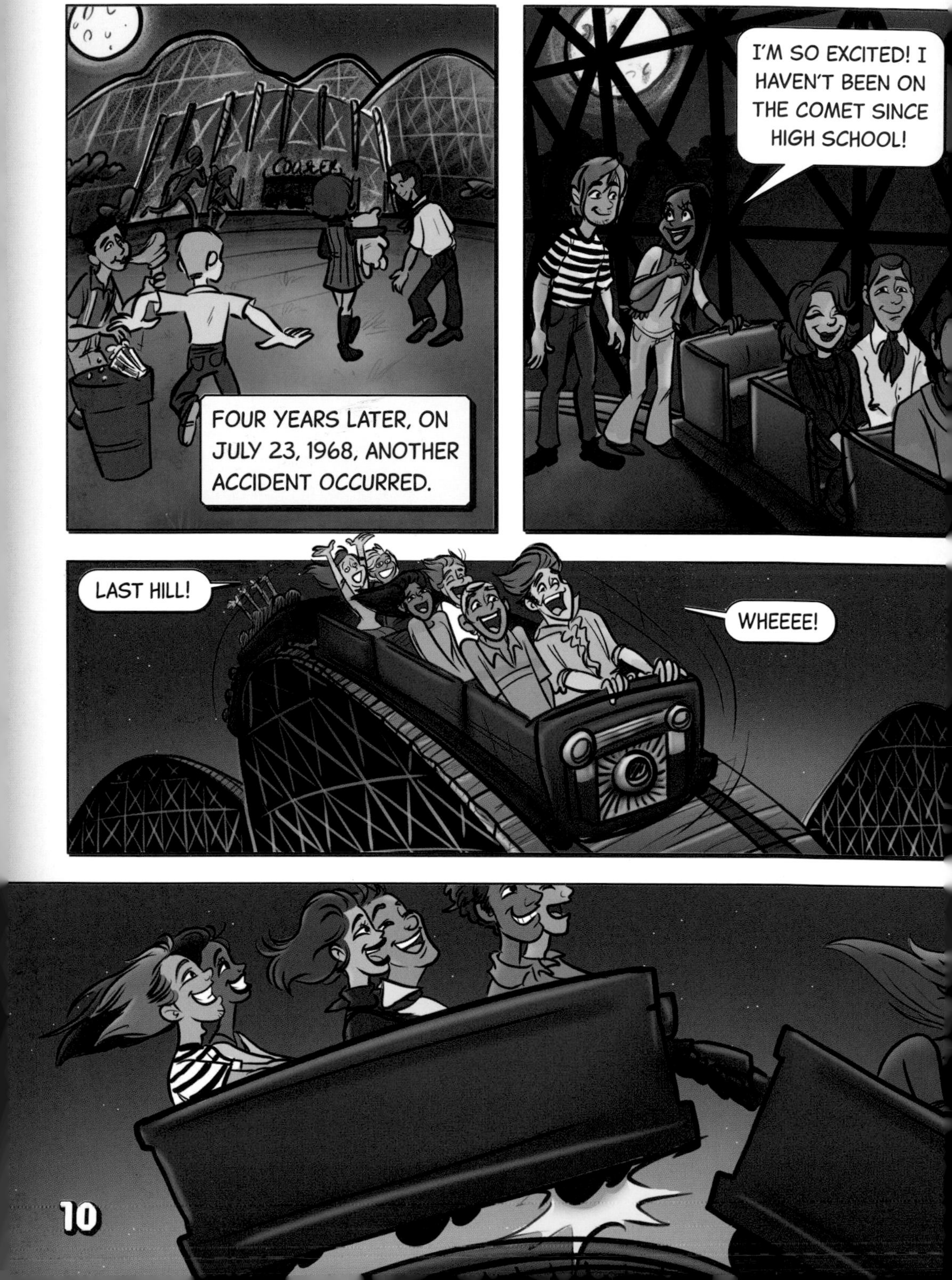

FOUR YEARS LATER, ON JULY 23, 1968, ANOTHER ACCIDENT OCCURRED.
I'M SO EXCITED! I HAVEN'T BEEN ON THE COMET SINCE HIGH SCHOOL!
LAST HILL!
WHEEEE!

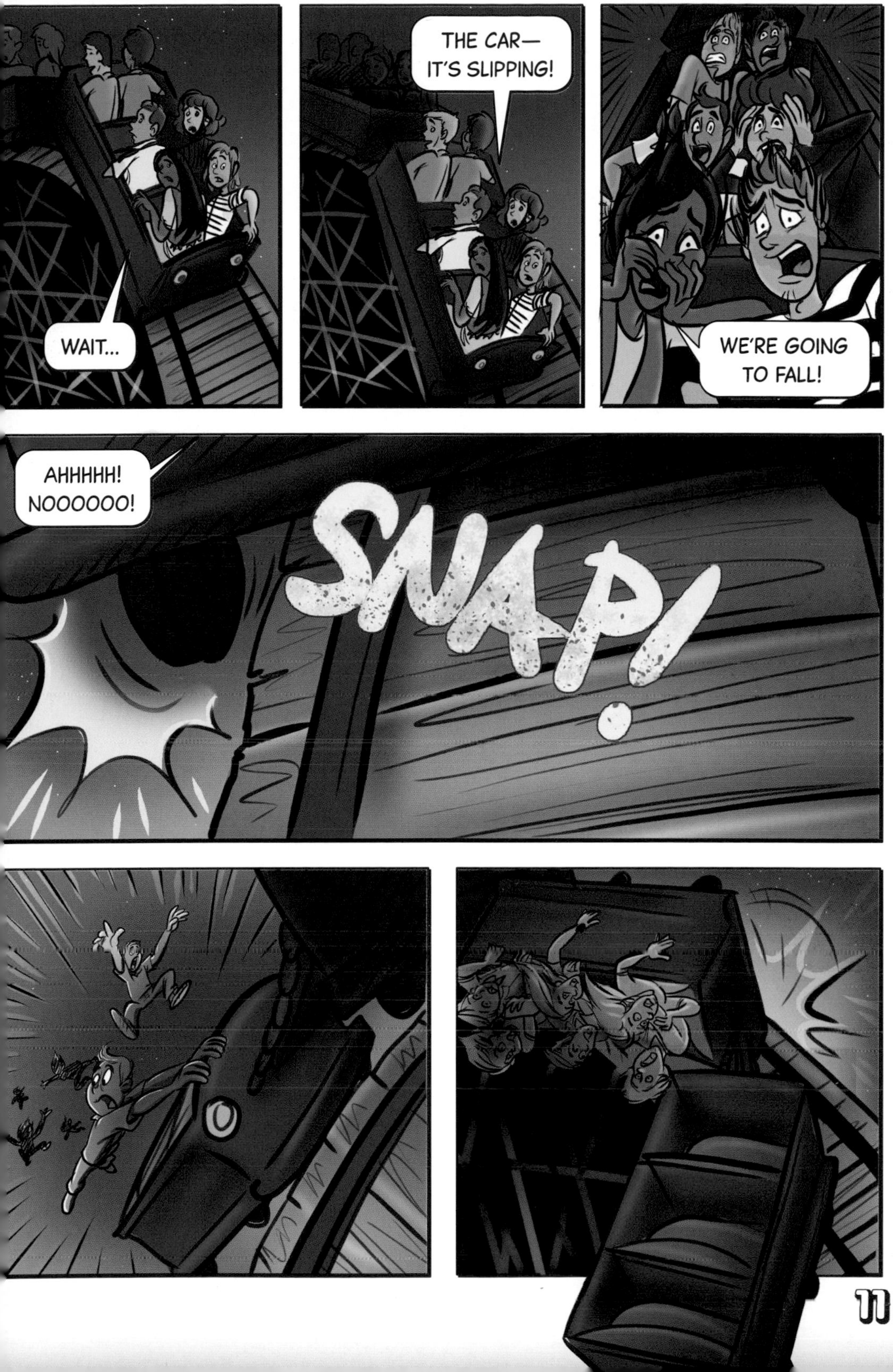
WAIT...
THE CAR— IT'S SLIPPING!
WE'RE GOING TO FALL!
AHHHHH! NOOOOOO!
SNAP!

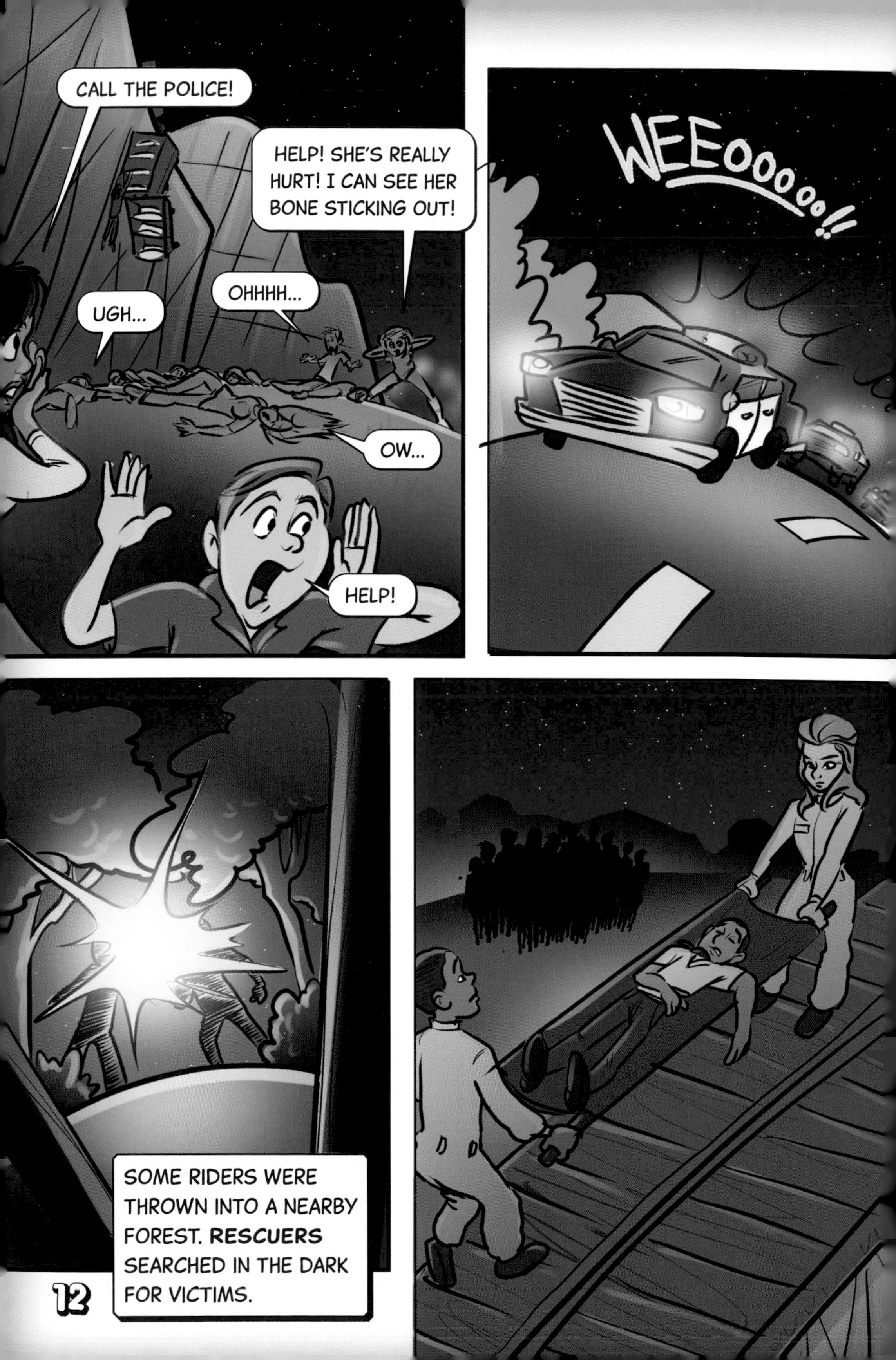
CALL THE POLICE!
HELP! SHE'S REALLY HURT! I CAN SEE HER BONE STICKING OUT!
UGH...
OHHHH...
OW...
HELP!
WEEOOOoo!!
SOME RIDERS WERE THROWN INTO A NEARBY FOREST. **RESCUERS** SEARCHED IN THE DARK FOR VICTIMS.

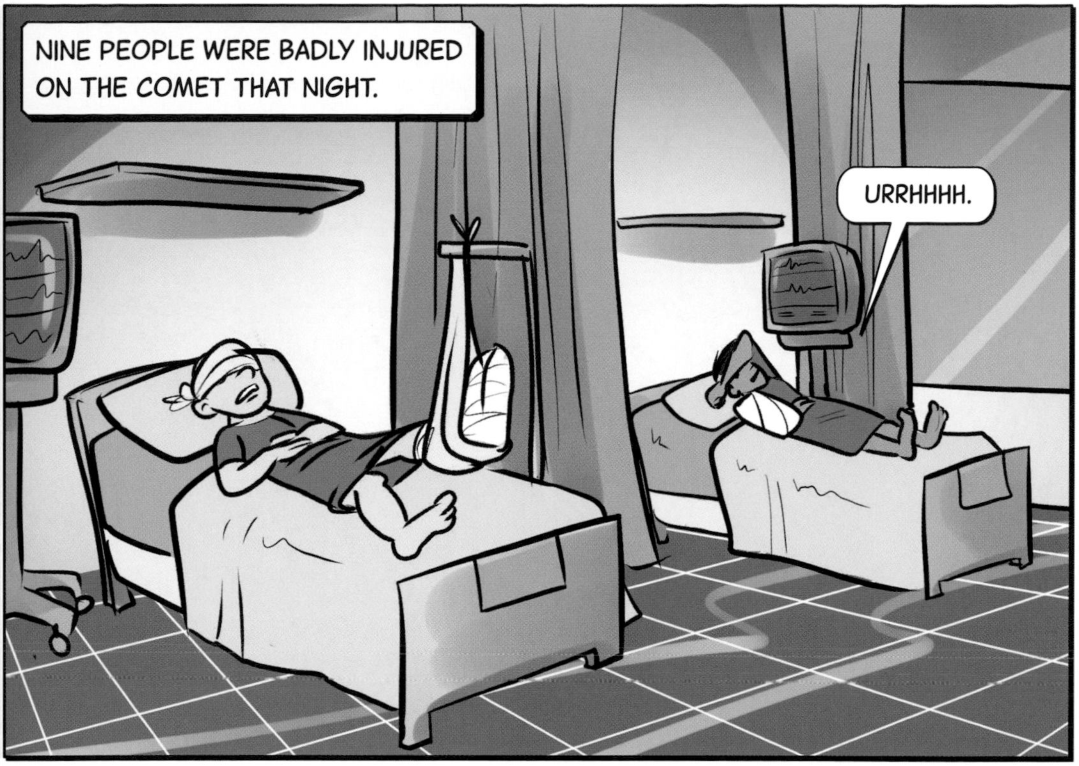
NINE PEOPLE WERE BADLY INJURED ON THE COMET THAT NIGHT.
URRHHHH.

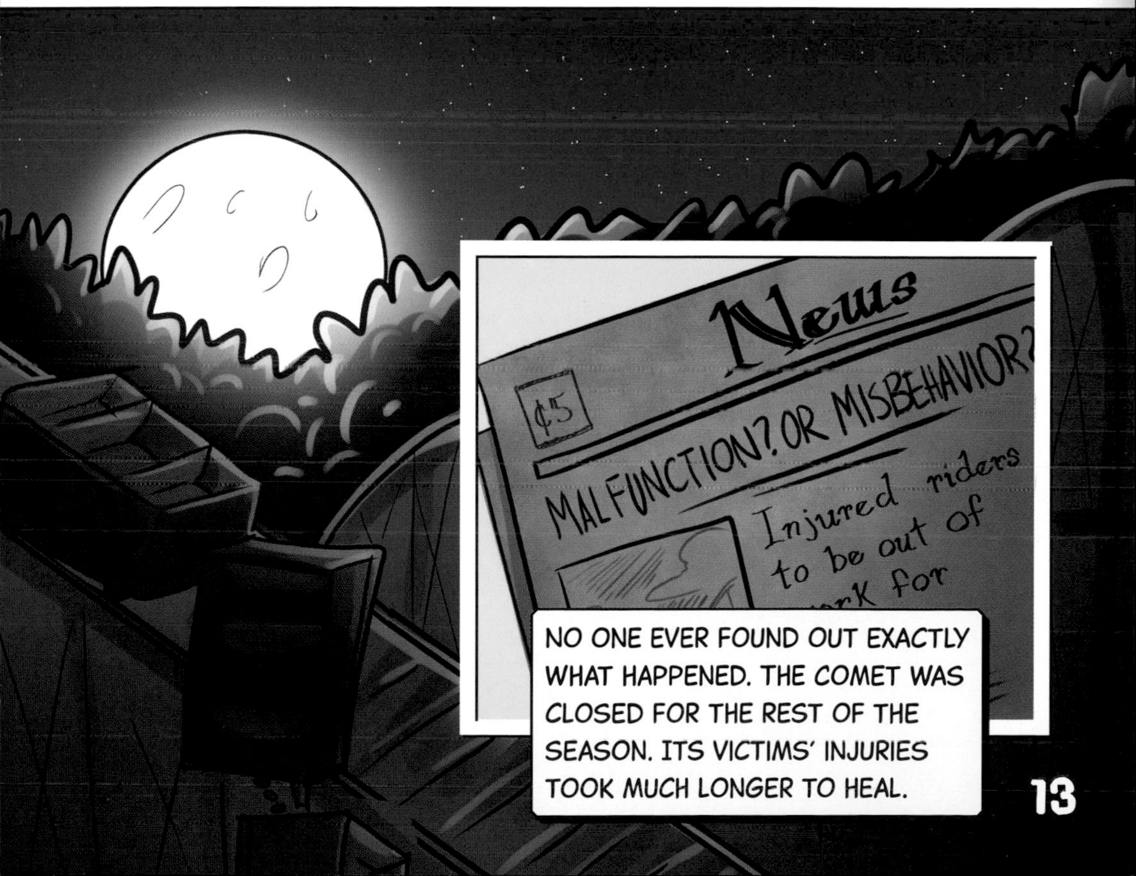
News
$5
MALFUNCTION? OR MISBEHAVIOR?
Injured riders to be out of
NO ONE EVER FOUND OUT EXACTLY WHAT HAPPENED. THE COMET WAS CLOSED FOR THE REST OF THE SEASON. ITS VICTIMS' INJURIES TOOK MUCH LONGER TO HEAL.

THE END OF THE COMET

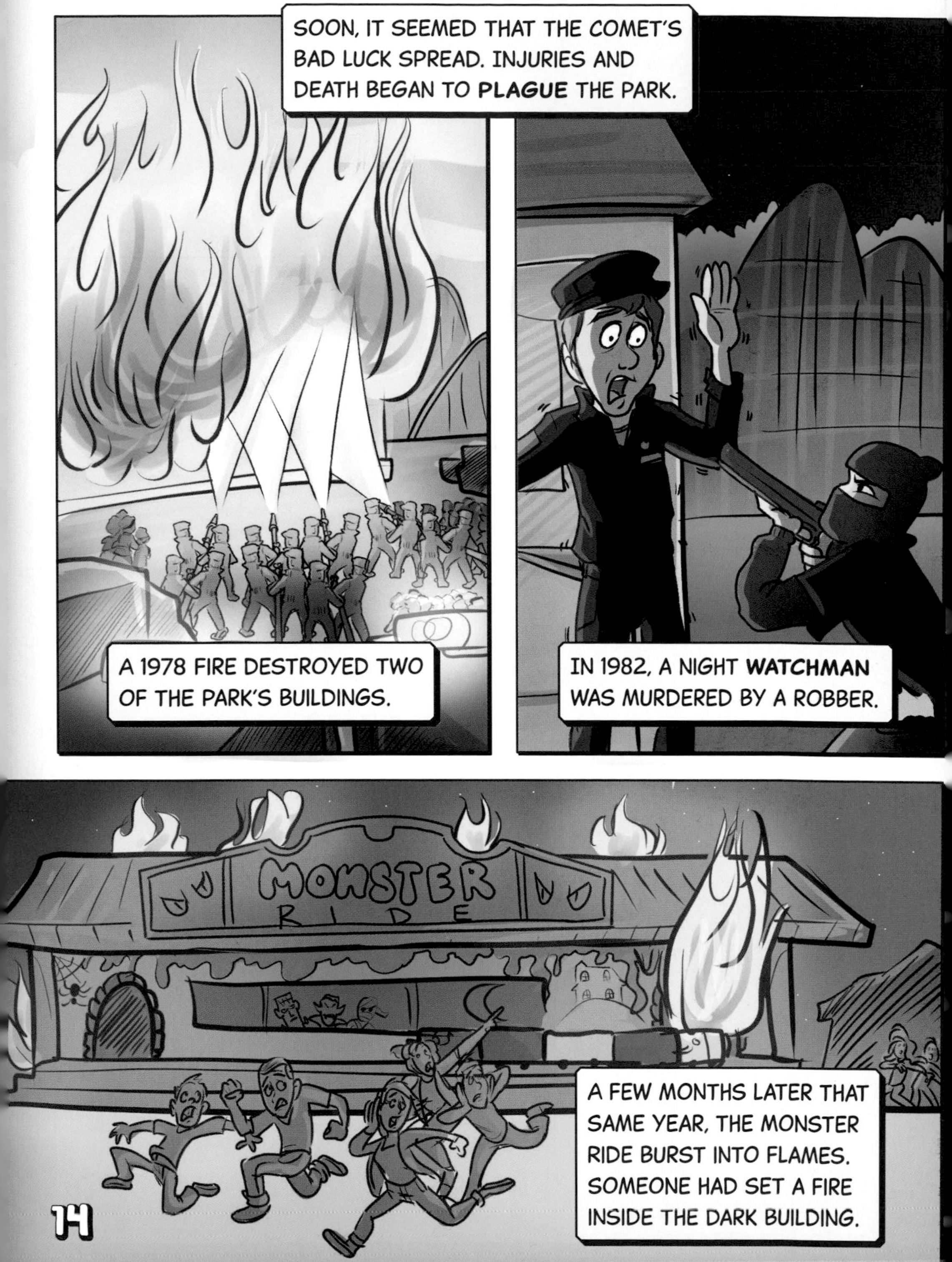
SOON, IT SEEMED THAT THE COMET'S BAD LUCK SPREAD. INJURIES AND DEATH BEGAN TO **PLAGUE** THE PARK.
A 1978 FIRE DESTROYED TWO OF THE PARK'S BUILDINGS.
IN 1982, A NIGHT **WATCHMAN** WAS MURDERED BY A ROBBER.
MONSTER RIDE
A FEW MONTHS LATER THAT SAME YEAR, THE MONSTER RIDE BURST INTO FLAMES. SOMEONE HAD SET A FIRE INSIDE THE DARK BUILDING.

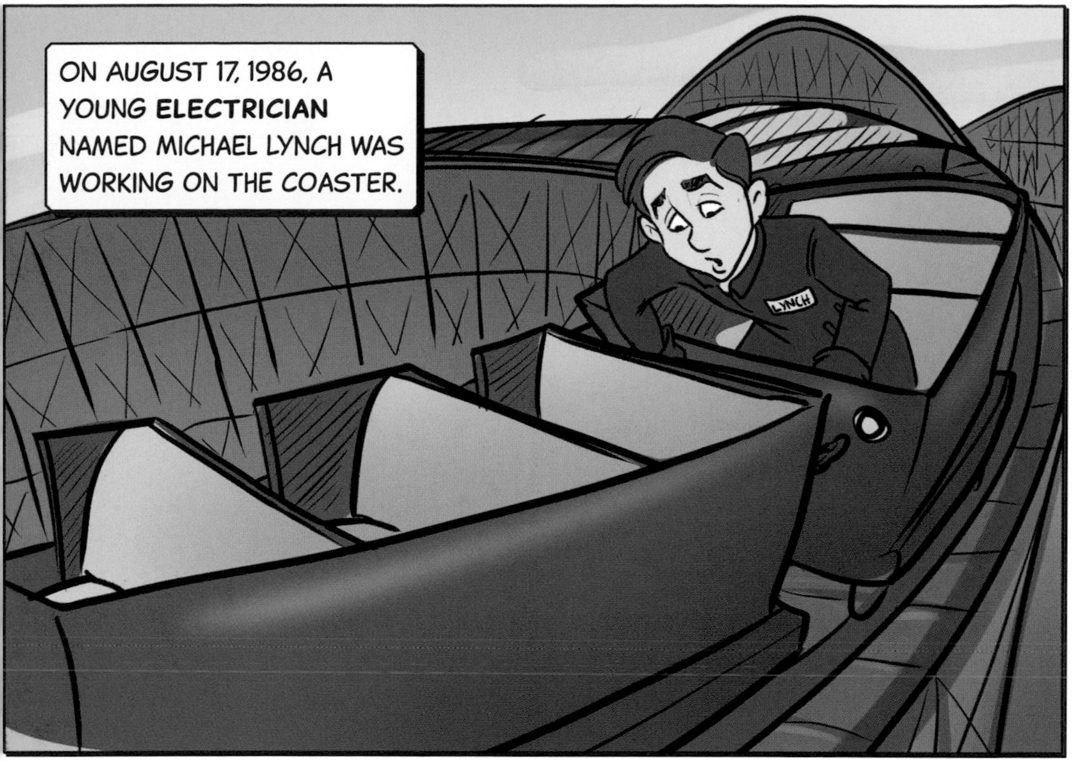
ON AUGUST 17, 1986, A YOUNG **ELECTRICIAN** NAMED MICHAEL LYNCH WAS WORKING ON THE COASTER.
LYNCH

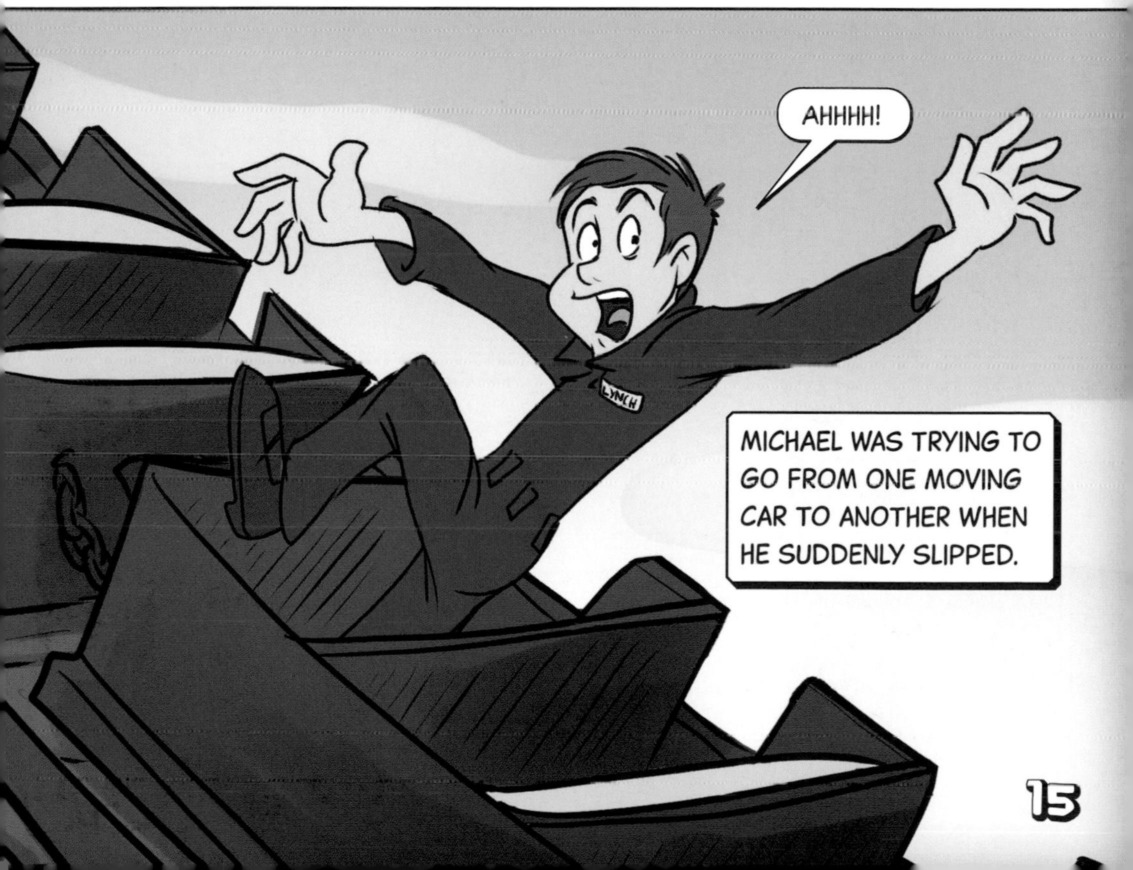
AHHHH!
LYNCH
MICHAEL WAS TRYING TO GO FROM ONE MOVING CAR TO ANOTHER WHEN HE SUDDENLY SLIPPED.

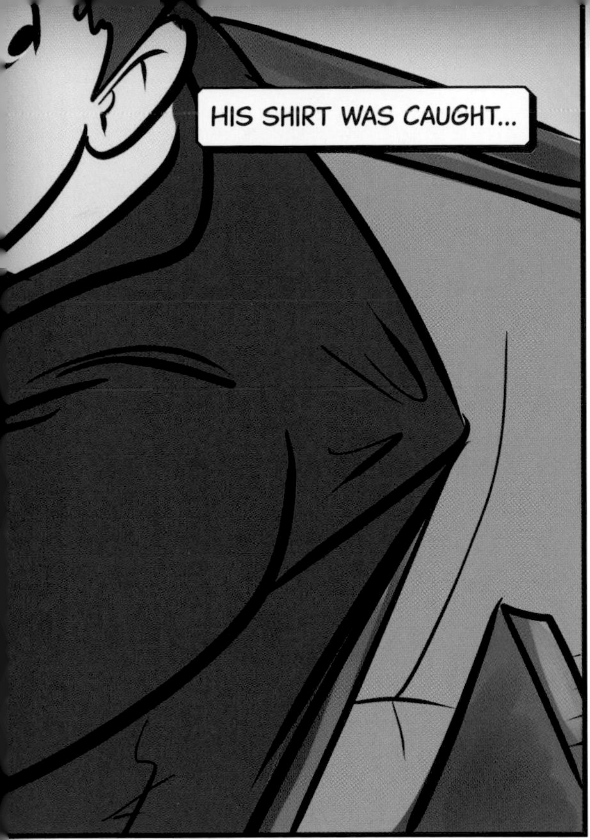
HIS SHIRT WAS CAUGHT...

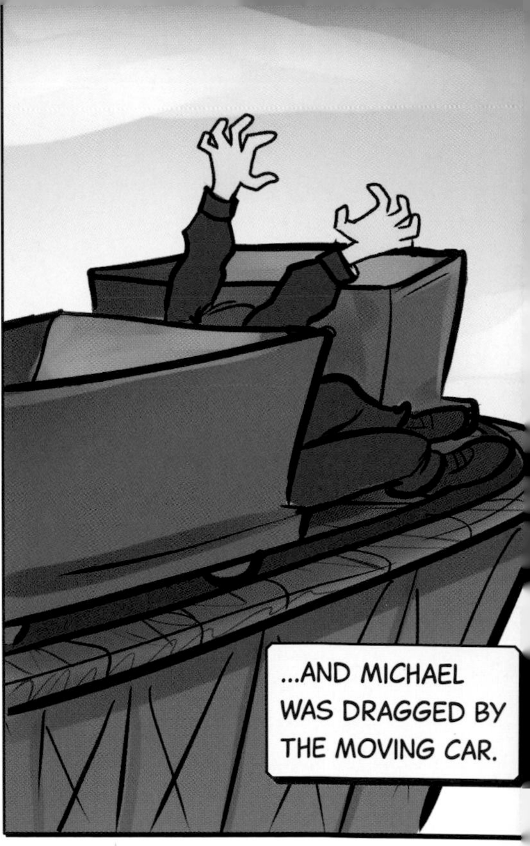
...AND MICHAEL WAS DRAGGED BY THE MOVING CAR.

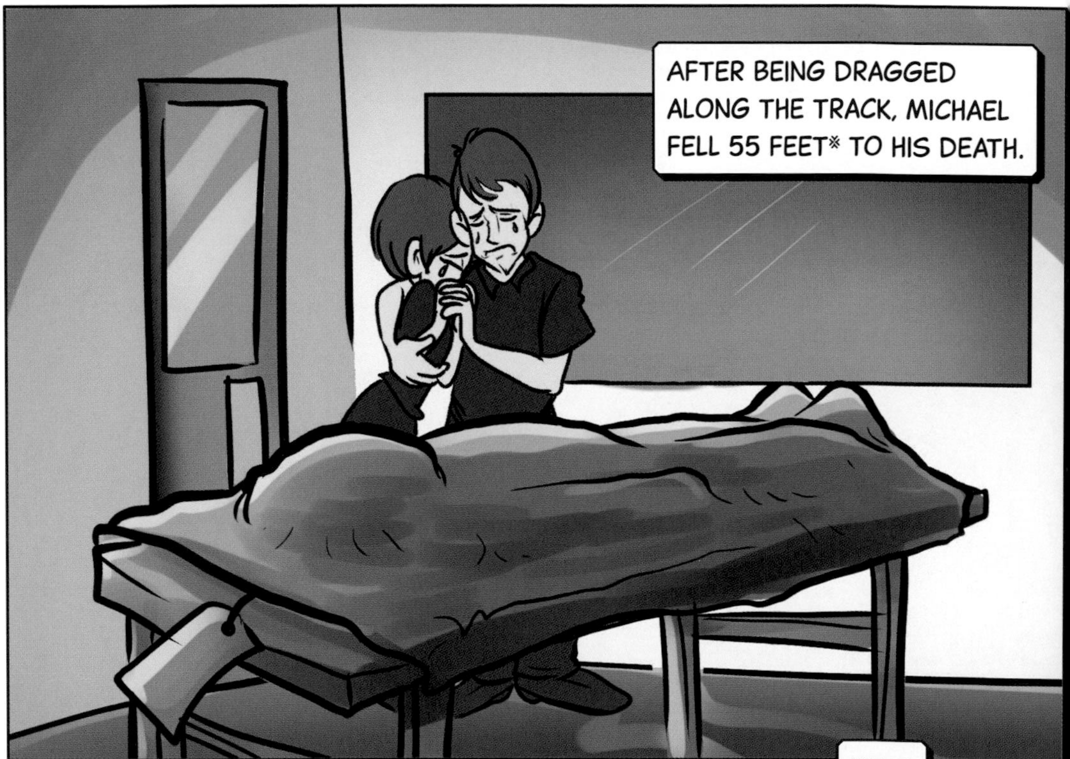
AFTER BEING DRAGGED ALONG THE TRACK, MICHAEL FELL 55 FEET※ TO HIS DEATH.
※17 M

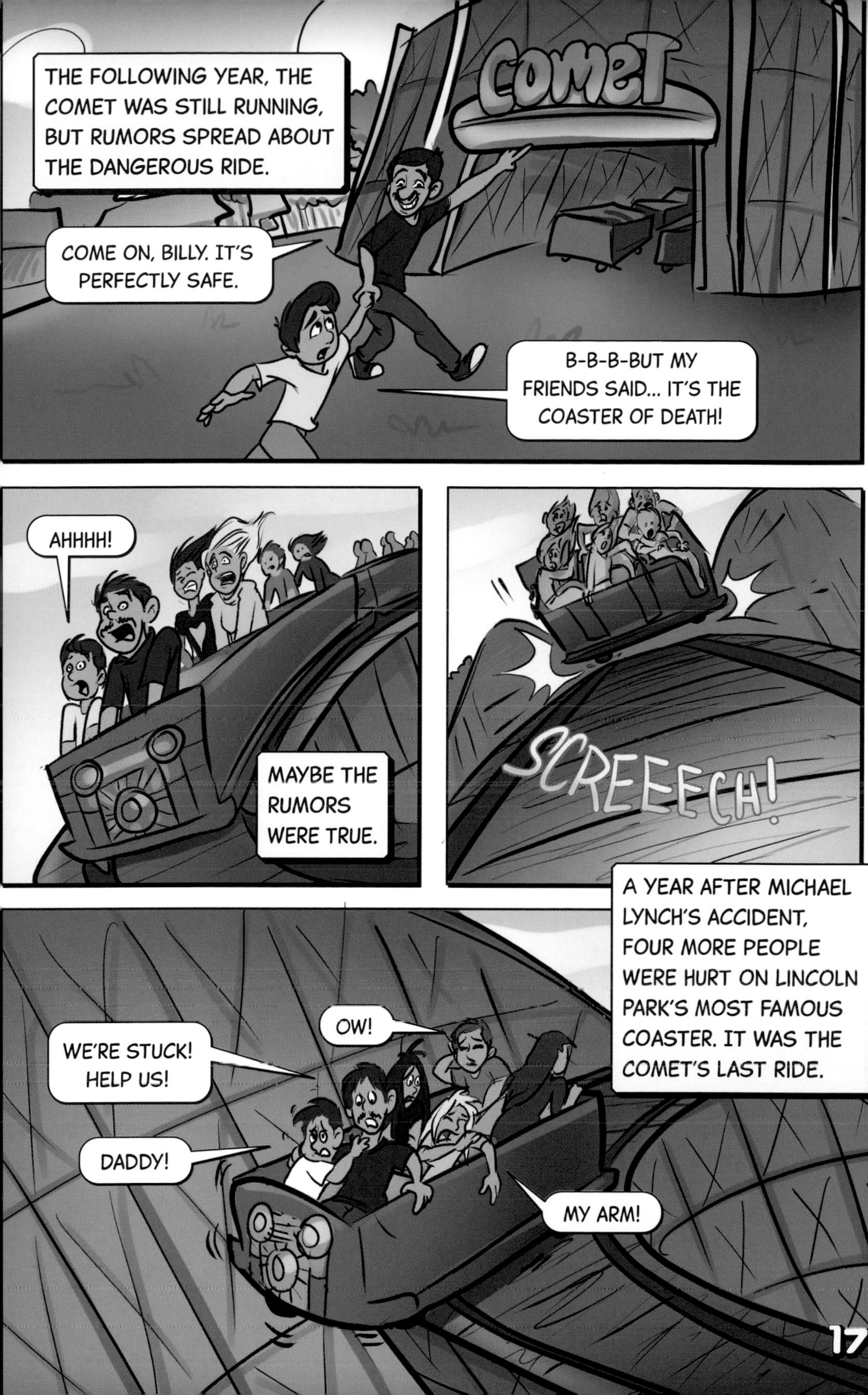
THE FOLLOWING YEAR, THE COMET WAS STILL RUNNING, BUT RUMORS SPREAD ABOUT THE DANGEROUS RIDE.
COMET
COME ON, BILLY. IT'S PERFECTLY SAFE.
B-B-B-BUT MY FRIENDS SAID... IT'S THE COASTER OF DEATH!
AHHHH!
MAYBE THE RUMORS WERE TRUE.
SCREEECH!
A YEAR AFTER MICHAEL LYNCH'S ACCIDENT, FOUR MORE PEOPLE WERE HURT ON LINCOLN PARK'S MOST FAMOUS COASTER. IT WAS THE COMET'S LAST RIDE.
OW!
WE'RE STUCK! HELP US!
DADDY!
MY ARM!

ABANDONED, BUT NOT GONE

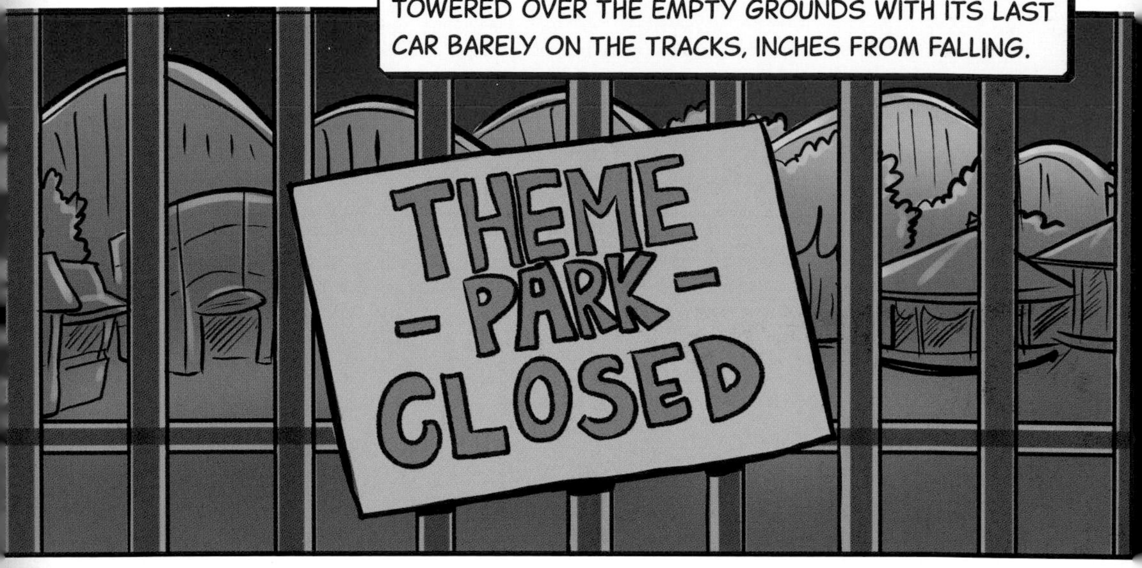
LINCOLN PARK CLOSED IN 1987. THE COMET STILL TOWERED OVER THE EMPTY GROUNDS WITH ITS LAST CAR BARELY ON THE TRACKS, INCHES FROM FALLING.
THEME - PARK - CLOSED

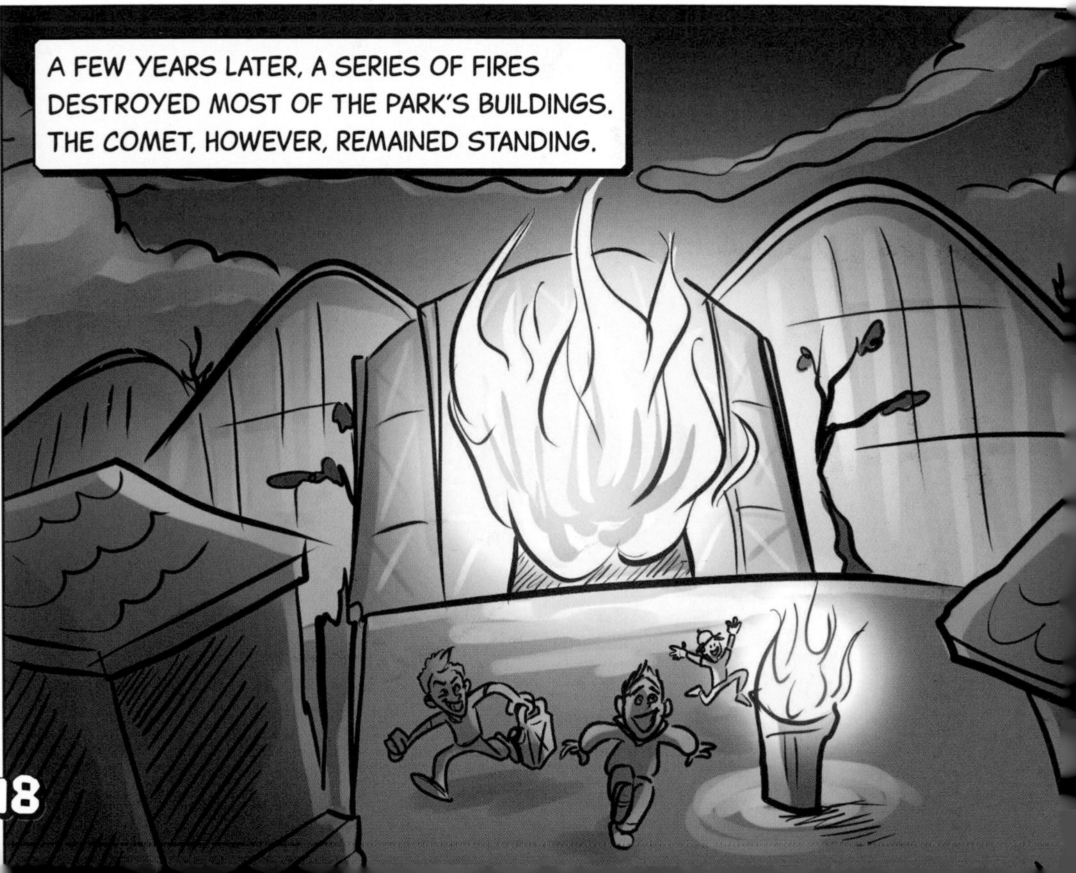
A FEW YEARS LATER, A SERIES OF FIRES DESTROYED MOST OF THE PARK'S BUILDINGS. THE COMET, HOWEVER, REMAINED STANDING.

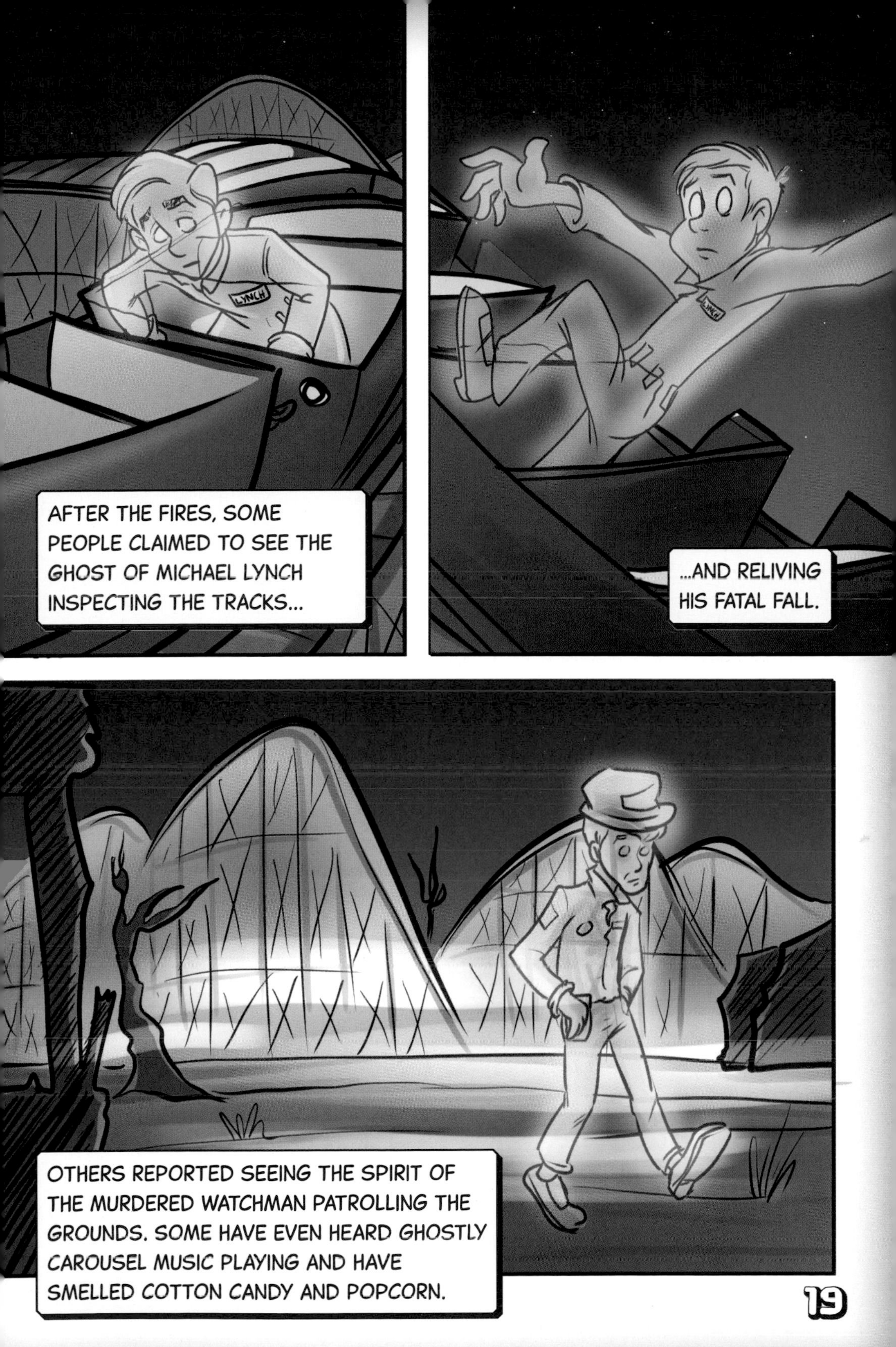
LYNCH
AFTER THE FIRES, SOME PEOPLE CLAIMED TO SEE THE GHOST OF MICHAEL LYNCH INSPECTING THE TRACKS...
LYNCH
...AND RELIVING HIS FATAL FALL.
OTHERS REPORTED SEEING THE SPIRIT OF THE MURDERED WATCHMAN PATROLLING THE GROUNDS. SOME HAVE EVEN HEARD GHOSTLY CAROUSEL MUSIC PLAYING AND HAVE SMELLED COTTON CANDY AND POPCORN.

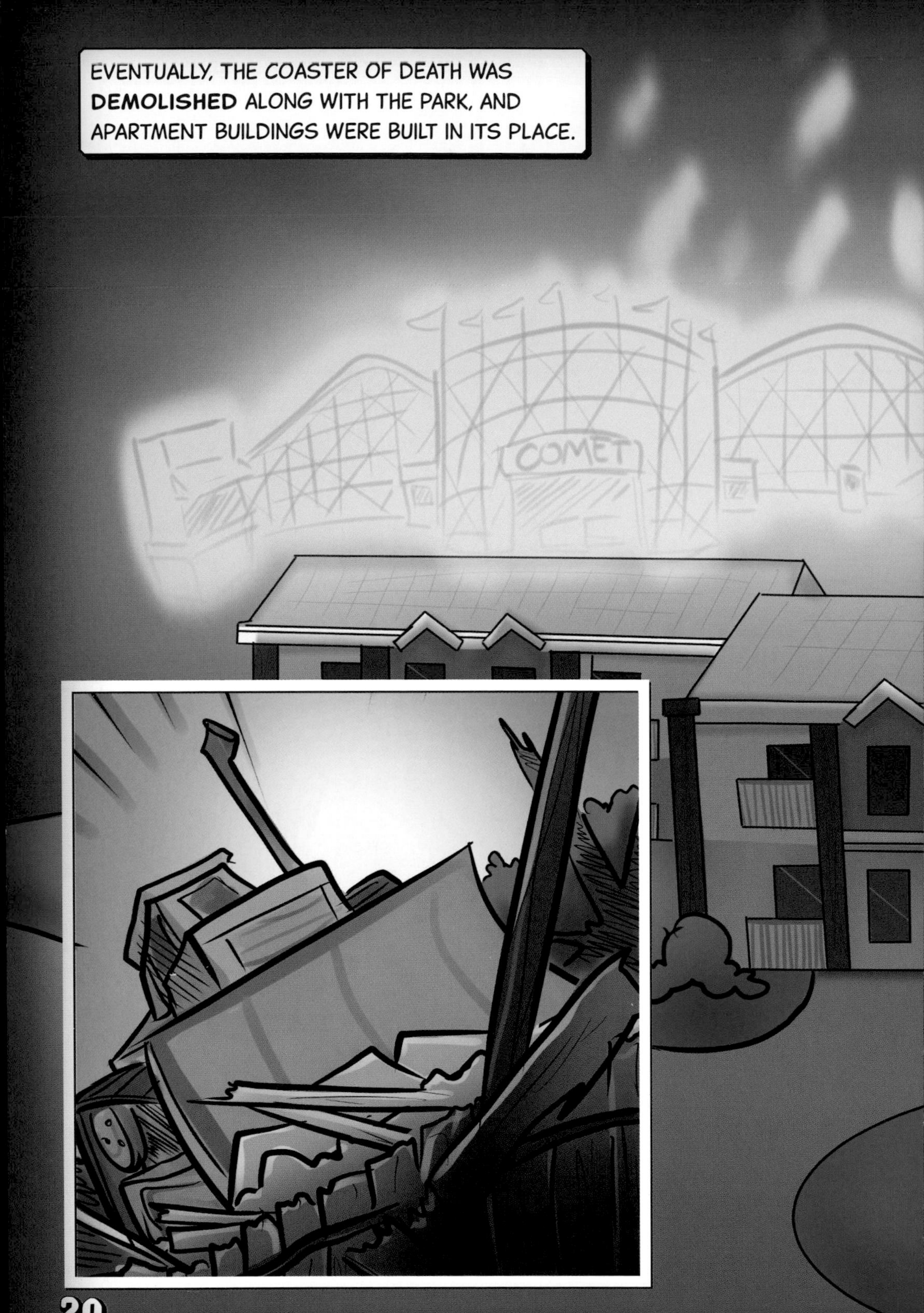
EVENTUALLY, THE COASTER OF DEATH WAS **DEMOLISHED** ALONG WITH THE PARK, AND APARTMENT BUILDINGS WERE BUILT IN ITS PLACE.
COMET

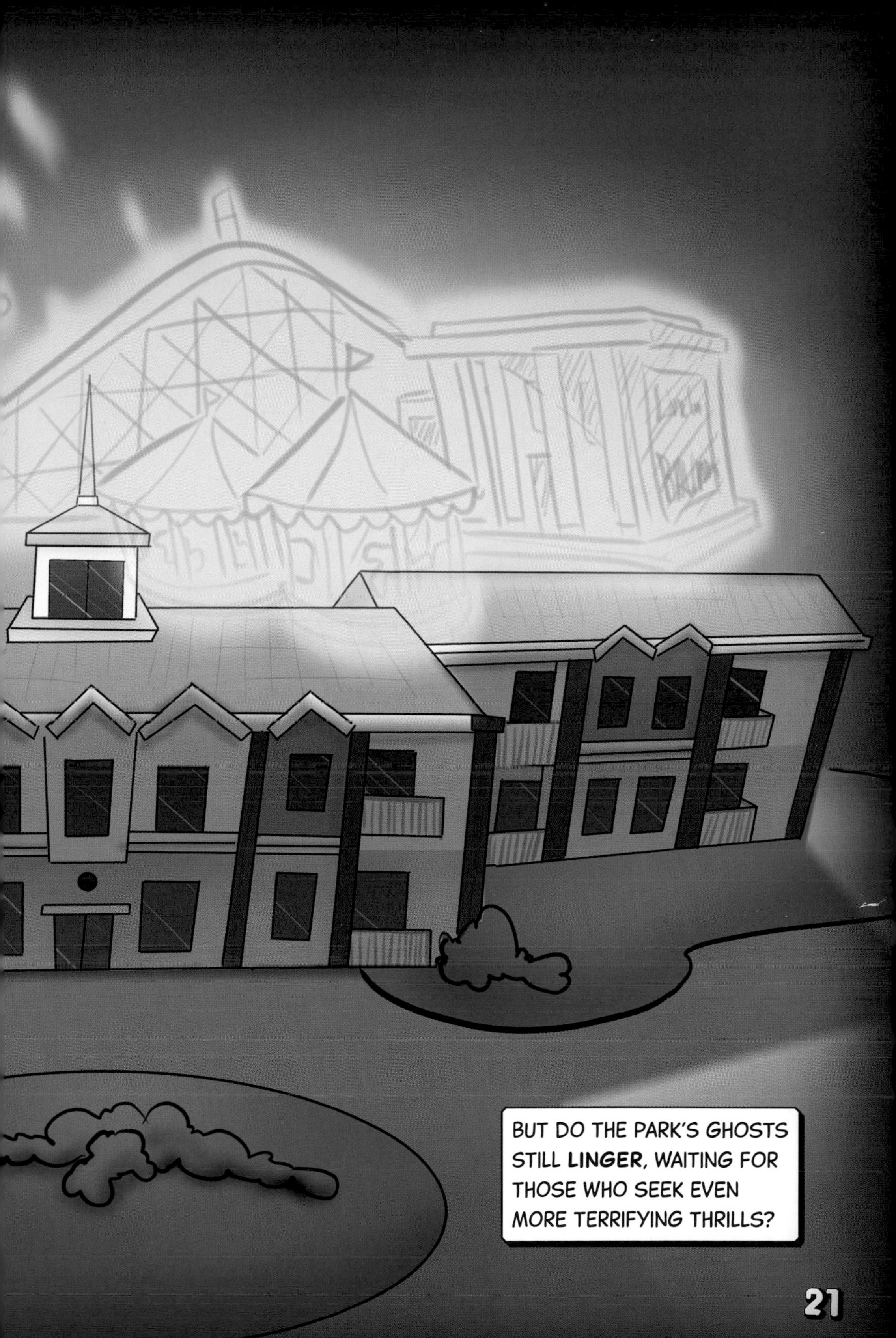
BUT DO THE PARK'S GHOSTS STILL **LINGER**, WAITING FOR THOSE WHO SEEK EVEN MORE TERRIFYING THRILLS?

OTHER SCARY
AMUSEMENT PARKS

PRIPYAT AMUSEMENT PARK
PRIPYAT, UKRAINE

Visitors enjoyed the Ferris wheel and the bumper cars at Pripyat Amusement Park. But not for long. The park was only a few miles away from the Chernobyl **nuclear power** plant. An explosion at the plant sent clouds of poisonous smoke into the air. Pripyat stayed open only one day until **residents** were told to leave. Years later, the Ferris wheel still sits empty, waiting for riders to climb aboard.

ELECTRIC PARK
KANSAS CITY, MISSOURI

When Electric Park opened, its buildings and towers blazed with the brightness of 100,000 lights. When it closed almost 20 years later, it was still **ablaze**. Only this time, it was lit up with yellow and orange flames! The park caught fire in 1925, and most of it was reduced to ashes.

GLOSSARY

ablaze on fire

accidents unplanned events that cause damage or injury

concessions stand a small shop where food is sold

demolished when a building or other structure has been knocked down

electrician a person who works on electrical equipment

linger to stay longer than expected

nuclear power a type of energy that is produced by splitting atoms

plague to cause someone or something trouble or suffering

rescuers people who save someone who is in danger

residents people who live in a certain place

tragedy a sad and terrible event

watchman a person who guards a building or property

INDEX

READ MORE

Andrus, Aubre, Megan Cooley Peterson, and Ebony Joy Wilkins. *Real-Life Ghost Stories: Spine-Tingling True Tales.* North Mankato, MN: Capstone Press (2020).

Claybourne, Anna. *Don't Read This Book Before Bed: Thrills, Chills, and Hauntingly True Stories.* Washington, DC: National Geographic (2017).

Taylor, Troy. *Creepy Libraries (Scary Places).* New York: Bearport Publishing (2018).

LEARN MORE ONLINE

1. Go to **www.factsurfer.com**

2. Enter "**Coaster of Death**" into the search box.

3. Click on the cover of this book to see a list of websites.